Memoirs of

The Mad Hatter

Nygel Stevenson

Published by

Dayglo Books Ltd, Nottingham, UK

www.dayglobooks.co.uk

0018-15-1419-01

© Nygel Stevenson 2015

The right of Nygel Stevenson to be identified as the author of this work has been asserted by him in accordance with the Designs and Copyright Act 1988.

Cover artwork & illustrations by
www.valentineart.co.uk

Typeset in Opendyslexic
by Abelardo Gonzales (2013)

Printed by IngramSpark

Distributed by Filament Publishing Ltd, Croydon

This book is subject to international copyright and may not be copied in any way without the prior written permission of the publishers.

Memoirs of
The Mad Hatter

Chapter 1

I am a happy man. Every day of my working life I've made it fun. Starting at the age of 13, with an after-school job as a butcher's boy, right up to now, as 'The Mad Hatter', I've gone to work every day and enjoyed it.

Madhatters Tea Shop is on two floors in a wonderful old building here in Kimberley, Nottingham, that at one time was the local Co-op.

I have customers who can remember it as it was then.

There were overhead wires that used to carry cash and change from the counter to the cashier's little booth in the corner.

That booth has gone but we still have lots of the original fitments. The counter, for instance, and glass-fronted cases on the walls and stacks of drawers and shelves.

So it's a quaint old place. I don't think the alterations we've made to turn it into a tea shop have spoiled the atmosphere.

In fact, after being used for years for other purposes, I like to think the Co-op people from the old days would be glad to see tea and coffee and cake being sold over the counter again.

Madhatters tea shop didn't start here. It began life across the road on Main Street and moved here to James Street in February 2015.

I hadn't really intended to open a café but a friend phoned me and said: "There's a coffee shop for sale on Main Street," so I walked up with the dog to have a look.

I'd never been in it, but I knew it had once been a butcher's shop, before the rebuilding was done.

It was now set up as a coffee shop but it hadn't been successful and had closed.

Anyway, I rang them and went to have a look inside.

When I told friends I was considering taking it, some people said it was in the wrong place, people wouldn't come, I wouldn't get the customers in.

But I liked the look of it.

So I trusted my instinct. I said: "Yes, I'll have it."

I signed all the paperwork and got the keys and moved in and that was a turning point for me.

I'd been up in Blackpool and I was sat around a table with some entertainer friends, one of them being Frank Carson.

He said: "What are you doing now?"

And I said: "I've just bought a coffee shop."

Frank turned round to me and said:

"You're as mad as a hatter! Buying a coffee shop and thinking you can start up a business in a recession."

I looked at him and said:

"You've just named my business."

He said: "What do you mean?"

I said: "I'm going to call it Madhatters."

I wanted a name that could be applicable to anything within the catering industry.

The tag line 'Madhatters – taste of perfection' could have applied to anything.

At that point I didn't know whether it was going to be a coffee shop or not. It might have been a deli or anything. I really wasn't sure what it was going to turn out to be.

I couldn't be sure it was going to work as a coffee shop – after all, the previous coffee shop hadn't done well there.

So although I knew I was on to something,

I didn't know for sure how it would turn out until we opened the doors.

That first week we hit the gravel, I knew it would be the best thing I'd ever done.

Chapter 2

That's over three years ago now, and the rest is history.

I've spent three years getting to know people, working with people, getting involved in the community.

I've got involved with all the local schools, judging competitions with the children, like cake baking and hat competitions. We've done dressing up and storytelling.

A huge pat on the back for me was to be asked to be a co-opted governor at one of the local primary schools. I just love doing that, seeing the children at school, getting involved with what they're doing. They're like sponges, just wanting to learn. It's wonderful.

We won the 'Mamma's and Pappa's' award as the most child-friendly eatery in Nottingham, which was huge.

We got to Number One out of over a thousand tea shops on Trip Advisor for Nottingham, and we're still in the top twenty.

It's hard work because you get positive and you get negative comments. You try to please everybody but it doesn't always happen. But you do your best.

After three years, the trouble with the original tea shop was the size – we only had the ground floor and there was no room to expand.

Before I moved to Kimberley, I came over on a visit and we went to pick up a take-away. We parked on James Street and I looked across at this building and I said: "That would make the most amazing antique shop."

I put it out of my mind because I couldn't do anything about it – it was already in use as a business.

After I'd opened the tea shop Jackie, a friend of mine, told me she knew Mike and Tessa who own that building. They were trying to rent it out as offices. Jackie introduced us.

I got to know them and literally almost bullied them into opening it as an antique shop.

The shop opened over a year ago as 'Alice's Antiques, Crafts & Collectables'.

It's full of the most amazing collection of original things for sale and, of course, the stock changes all the time so it's always interesting.

Mike and Tessa agreed to work alongside Madhatter's, so we could promote the two businesses together.

When the three-year lease was up at the old shop, I decided the best thing to do was talk to Mike and Tessa and see if we could work together even more closely.

So the Mad Hatter and Alice had their 'engagement' and then the 'marriage' of the two took place in February 2015 when we moved in to 'Alice's'.

In truth, I don't think Mike and Tessa knew what had hit them. While the builders were constructing the kitchen and a disabled loo on the ground floor, there was a procession of people carrying boxes up the hill from the old shop.

As well as all the furniture and equipment, and all the hats people had given us, of course, we moved a total of over a thousand cups and saucers – and we never broke one!

I really must stop buying tea sets. But I just can't resist temptation!

So now we have two floors of tea rooms and unique shopping together in 'Alice's'. It's a real 'wonderland' and everybody loves it.

Ever since we started we have been lucky to attract a lot of positive publicity. We've been featured in newspapers and magazines – 'Readers Digest' was a big one.

I've been on local radio and we've even had TV cameras in the shop.

What I love, especially, is that we employ local people, give them an opportunity and a stepping stone. Staff come and go. While they're here they have fun and then they go and move on to their next project.

Many of the staff are young, so I expect them to move on. It's like a family. In fact, I think of the business as a family – you expect your children to move on.

We have up to ten staff now, which is fantastic. It's thriving and it keeps us all busy.

My hard-working staff with well-earned Trip Advisor Certificate of Excellence

READER'S DIGEST

Madhatter's
NOTTINGHAM

Madhatter's owner Nygel Stevenson invites his guests to "enter the Wonderland" at his quirky cafe in Kimberley, Nottingham. Tea, coffee and cake are served against a backdrop inspired by Lewis Carroll's novel—and customers are invited to choose from a selection of hats as they take part in their very own Madhatter's tea party.

The emphasis is on creating a welcoming, child-friendly environment, and it's one that's gone down well—customers have voted it into the top ten places to eat in Nottingham.

■ **Visit madhattersshop.co.uk for details**

Where do you go to enjoy tea or coffee? If we haven't mentioned it here, tell us about it by emailing readersletters@readersdigest.co.uk

11•2014 | 65

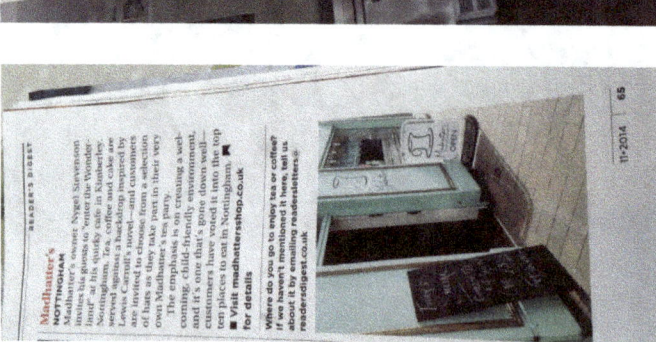

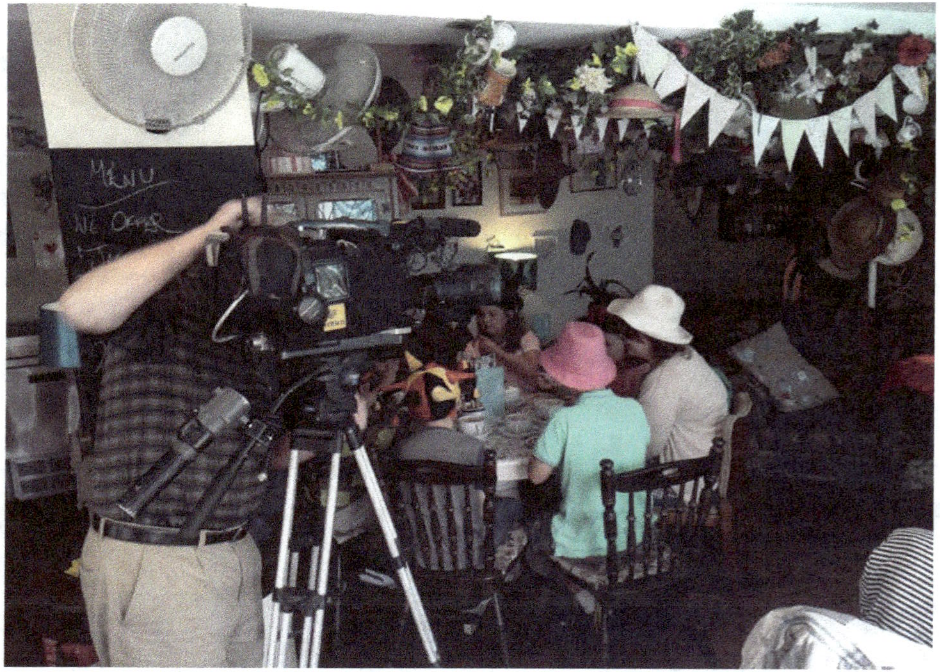

The print media and TV love Madhatters. Can't show you the radio coverage, sadly!

Staff visit to the Houses of Parliament, at the invitation of our MP, Anna Soubry

The Mad Hatter with other local business proprietors – who also love hats!

Chapter 3

When I was a young teenager, I was struggling with who I was, what I was, where I was coming from. I didn't know what the word 'gay' meant but I kept being called it all the time.

I remember the Headmaster calling me into his office and he said: "Well, Nygel, are you gay? Do you need help?" and I still didn't get what he meant.

It was a very different way of counselling and talking back then. I just didn't talk to my parents about it, or anybody, because I didn't know what I was dealing with.

It wasn't until I'd moved away from home, then I realised what was happening.

I grew up with my two sisters and we had a wonderful childhood. We lived a delightful village life and it was a happy family.

My sisters and me used to go down to the village and feed apples to the horses. It was an idyllic childhood in many ways.

Sunday mornings it was off to Sunday school, then taken out for trips in the car in the afternoon with grandparents or mum and dad.

I remember days out to Dovedale, going over the Snape Pass, having a picnic, having an ice cream. They were just lovely family days out.

And we had great family holidays in a farmhouse in Devon.

I went to private school. I started at a private nursery and then a private primary school and then private senior school.

To this day, I know that being in private education has helped me in my day-to-day life – by having a structure, by having the strictness and the discipline.

And because a lot of the people there were from a wealthy background. They came from families who had a Bentley or a Rolls. They had pots of money. They had houses with loads of bedrooms. They went skiing. Mixing with my rich schoolmates gave me the confidence to move very easily among those sort of people.

I can get on with absolutely anyone from any background.

Chapter 4

Going into the teenage phase – around 13 or 14 – I used to escape down to London. I would take myself on a National Express coach down to London on a Saturday morning and I'd use my spending money to take myself to the theatre.

I remember the first time I ever did that, I didn't tell anyone what I was doing. I went to see "Aspects of Love" with Michael Ball.

I'll never forget going to see that. I was 13.

I phoned my mum and said: "Would you like anything from London, Mum?" and she said "What are you talking about?"

She went absolutely ballistic. When I got back to Nottingham Victoria bus station my Dad was waiting there to pick me up. Did I get told off for doing that!

But they were all right about it afterwards. They let me do trips to London on my own.

When I was 15 they actually paid for a coach trip for me to go to Belgium on my own. That wouldn't be allowed nowadays.

But that was how I got the bug for London. I thought it was wonderful, this amazing place. The glamour and the history. That's where it all happened. It excited me and it still does.

It's such a big city. I still get it, if I'm driving down to London. As soon as I see Brent Cross I start to get excited. If you go on the train, coming into St Pancras you get excited, don't you?

I moved to London when I was 20. I was a year ahead at school, so I did my A-levels at 17. I finished school in the June and I had a job to go to, starting in the September. It was a Retail Management Traineeship at The John Lewis Partnership.

I decided that to fill in the time during the summer I would like to do some work in a hotel. So I got the yellow pages and just started ringing round hotels to see if someone would take me on. I found one that I liked the sound of called 'The Waltons'.

I rang them up and I went and saw the lady there. I didn't know a thing about catering but she said: "Right, okay, I'll give you a trial." So I started right away and worked there the whole summer and absolutely loved it.

Then I went to work for John Lewis. But I loved the hotel job so much that I carried on working at the hotel on Sundays. In fact, 'The Waltons' started serving Sunday lunch so that I could stay on, serving the Sunday lunch customers. So I did Tuesday to Saturday at John Lewis and Sunday at the hotel.

After a year at John Lewis I realised that I hated retail. It wasn't for me. So I went back to the hotel full time.

And they said you need to learn this business thoroughly. We need to get you off to

London for you to go and start your professional journey.

So I moved down to London and got a job at a wine merchant's and signed up with an agency. So that's how catering arrived in my life – by accident, really.

When I first went to London I was very organised. I got the job at the wine merchant's through the 'Catering & Hotelkeeper' magazine.

Then it was a matter of finding somewhere to live. So I drove down to London with a friend to try to find some accommodation.

We walked all over the place, looking at Estate Agents but I just couldn't afford anywhere. The wages that I was going to be on wouldn't pay for a broom cupboard in London.

We went for a coffee at this coffee shop on Knightsbridge, at the side of the Berkeley Hotel. Gordon Ramsey's restaurant is there now. It was called The Minema Cinema.

The people who had designed it designed airline cabins and all that sort of stuff. The staircase had drawers in all the steps – things like that. Everything was so compact. I was absolutely fascinated, talking to this girl who worked there.

I was chatting away to her and she said: "Where do you live?" So I explained to her that I was moving down to London and was looking for somewhere. And she told me about 'The P.M. Club' as it was called.

This was before mobile phones, so we went to a phone box and got the phone number and phoned them. Then we got on the tube and went over to Earl's Court and found 'The P.M. Club'.

They said yes, they could give me an application form. So I filled in the application and I was accepted.

It was originally 'The Prime Minister's Club' years and years ago. Basically, it was set up specifically as a hostel for people in the hotel and catering industry who needed a room. It started off at St.Martin's-in-the-Fields and then it moved out to Earl's Court, to Barkston Gardens.

It was a beautiful red brick, mansion building. My next-door-but-one neighbour was Twiggy. She's still there!

There was the boys' block and the girls' block. Initially it was a shared room and you put yourself on a waiting list for your own single room. I paid £35 a week for my room. It was the only way I could afford to live in London.

I still love London. It brings back happy memories of me finding out who I wanted to be and no one questioning me. Nobody labelling me. Nobody judging me. I was just allowed to be me.

But along with that went the loneliness. I wasn't judged but neither was I a part of anything. Alongside the freedom went having to be very self-sufficient.

Chapter 5

My job was in the City, Mondays to Fridays, and initially I'd come home on a Friday evening and go back on a Sunday night.

But I was getting more and more homesick. Then someone that I'd met at work said: "Don't go home at weekends. Stay here. Get to know London."

So I did. I got myself a job on Sundays in Baskins Robbins ice cream parlour on Earl's Court Road, just round the corner from where I lived.

However wild the Saturday night, however bad the hangover, I was there bright and early on Sunday morning, in my little pink and grey uniform and my little hat, doing fast counter service for people wanting pastries or ice cream for breakfast. And you would be surprised how many people in that part of London did!

And I walked. And I walked. And I walked. That's why I know London so well, because I just walked everywhere.

London suburbs are like a lot of little villages. They're all joined together and I'd walk from one to another and another.

One weekend I ended up at Heathrow Airport and had to get the tube back on the Piccadilly Line – I'd walked all the way there from Earl's Court.

When I moved to London I loved it because I could be anybody. At the same time, it could be extremely lonely. And that was a problem. I had spent all my time at school with people who were wealthy, and now I started to make believe that I was wealthy too.

I developed this spendthrift habit – keeping up with the Jones's, and almost buying friends, which you do when you're lonely.

I'd think: "Who can I ask out tonight? Who can I entertain?" I'd meet friends – well, I thought they were friends – and I'd say: "Oh, I'll pay for dinner" and we'd go to Soho and have a private room at 'L'Escargot' French restaurant.

There'd be twelve of us. I'd take everybody out because it was the way I could get friends.

I paid the price afterwards. Not everybody does, but I did, because I was quite a gregarious person.

And I had the means – or believed I did. There were plastic cards that were being thrown at me, all the time. You see money available to spend and you think it's yours, and you make these mistakes.

But I still had fun, great fun, and some of those people I still see or hear of, now. Some of them aren't around anymore.

I was always at the theatre and I got to know a lot of the theatre crowd. At the time, if you got to know the people at the stage door, you could sit with the sound engineer and watch the show. You just took the sound engineer a bottle of wine and a box of chocolates and you could sit in the sound box with him.

I used to see 'Phantom of the Opera' on regular occasions. Sometimes he'd let me press the button to bring the chandelier down. Oh! The power! Wouldn't you like to do that!

As my jobs got better and my wages got better, I was coming into the hostel in Barkston Gardens with my spendthrift Selfridges bags and Harrods bags.

I got pulled over by the manager one day. He said: "I think it's time you looked for somewhere else, Nygel, because the idea is that this is a cheap hostel for catering workers and by the look of it, you can afford to find your own place now."

Through one of the wine bars I'd been working in I had met this lady who was an actress. She was very eccentric. She was always 'resting'! She let me rent a room in her house. I think I still only paid about £50 a week. That was at Streatham Common in south London.

Living with this lady, we had parties and we had fun. I was getting up to mischief and doing things that are completely unrepeatable – I'd never want my parents to know about them!

I got into the naughty scene. I got into lavish spending, and the lavish life style. But we all make mistakes and I hope it didn't really change the person I am.

I also met a lot of people in the gay community. The one who made the biggest impression on me, without a doubt, was George

O'Dowd – Boy George – because of the way he stood for who he was, what he was, and he didn't care.

He's made mistakes. We've all made mistakes. But he's still that person that he was all those years ago. He's quite happy being who he is and creating a reaction.

I think, in the gay community, you're either loved or hated. That's the extreme. He inspired me and I have met him, and told him so.

I saw his musical because I love his music, but I also wanted to find out about his life and his kind of extreme behaviour, which I fell into – some parts of it – when I was in London.

You learn that it's not necessarily the right way but you've got to do it, to find out if it is the right way or the wrong way for you. He did inspire me.

Lots of people have, in many walks of life, who stand up for what they believe in, whatever they are, whoever they are.

Since I've been living here, I've just been me. I haven't labelled myself. Actually, I like the label 'The Mad Hatter' because I can hide behind that. The vast majority of people accept me as I am, because I'm harmless. I just do what I do, and enjoy life.

Chapter 6

At that time I had a day job in a wine bar in the City and I worked in the evenings and on my days off for an agency. They sent me absolutely anywhere, doing silver service waiting and drinks receptions.

I worked on The Orient Express, in The Royal Household, anywhere that I was sent. That was part of my mad London days.

I was doing a very big do for Parliament but it was at a property on Whitehall, linked to the back of The Banqueting House. I was asked to go through these double doors with a tray of drinks, to greet people on the other side.

So I got my tray of drinks, opened the door, walked through bold as brass, and wondered what this curtain was for.

I moved the curtain aside and there was the cat walk of The Banqueting House, with hundreds of people having a meal, waiting for the speaker to come on after dinner. They had played a practical joke on me!

So instead of walking straight back out, Nygel just burst into song. I sang "The sun will come out tomorrow". So that was a bit of fun and I got a round of applause!

In the hospitality industry you're looking

after people at every stage, from christenings, to weddings, to funerals, bar mitzvahs, everything. Most of the time people are having fun.

I can remember the first ever funeral I did. It was somebody I knew, which made it even harder. It was so difficult. I'll never forget that day.

You do everything you possibly can to make sure the food and drink are exactly right.

When people first come in they are very sad but then they have a few drinks and relax and start talking about the person and begin to have a laugh.

My job is always to try to make everybody happy, on every occasion. That was difficult. Funerals still are – they are hard work.

The most interesting place I ever worked was at a private party in London. It was on a crescented road, somewhere near Regent's Park.

It was to look after an elderly couple's wedding anniversary. There was a chef and I was the waiter and it was literally just the two of them. Their granddaughter had bought it as a present for them.

I waited on this couple for a whole evening and the stories they told me! They were seventy-five years married. They were absolutely incredible. Their house was like a museum.

That's where I got my love of things old and interesting and eclectic and complete. She was a real 'Barbara Cartland' type of character and he was like a sergeant major. They were chalk and cheese. I'll never forget that night. They had such fantastic tales.

You can talk about interesting places, but the most interesting thing is people. That sticks in my mind as the most interesting working job I've ever been sent to. I got so much from them, and particularly their togetherness. My grandparents were together for the same length of time.

Chapter 7

When I was sent to Buckingham Palace I had to sign the Official Secrets Act, so I'm not allowed to say too much! I was sent to the Palace on an agency job.

The first time I arrived, I was very nervous. I did clear the wrong plate when I cleared the queen's plate. Her knife and fork weren't together and I wasn't sure if she'd finished. She was talking to the person next to her and she ignored me. I was so nervous.

My nerves got the better of me and I said: "You can't have a pudding if you haven't eaten all your greens!" She turned round to me and said: "I've had quite sufficient, thank you. Just clear my plate."

I stood there and thought: "I'm going to be beheaded! I'm never going to be allowed to come back again."

Two weeks later I got a phone call asking me back. I went back to the Palace to do a drinks party.

While I was setting up all the glasses for the reception and getting everything ready, there was this old lady working in the room with me. She was someone from the florists. She was sitting at the top of a step ladder in a bay window, doing a flower display.

I relayed this story to her, telling her what

I'd done the first time I came to the palace, making a fool of myself.

After about fifteen minutes, this lady came down the step ladder. She smiled and said to me: "I shall go and make myself beautiful now," and she wasn't a florist – it was the queen!

She is head of the W.I. and the drinks reception was for them. They all had to bring a flower arrangement and she had been doing hers.

So that was quite interesting! It just shows that I don't mind who I talk to, or how I talk to them and everyone is equal. I think the queen appreciated that. Definitely.

I've always tried to be a good boy and do everything the right way, but sometimes I'm a little bit naughty. I can't help it.

I was sent to a job at a very, very posh house in Twickenham. I arrived and didn't like it. I didn't like the feel of the place. There was something not right about it.

I went in the front door, all suited and booted, and I thought: "This is not right for me."

The caterers asked me to go out to the shop to get something – lemons, I think it was. I went out of the back door, out of the back gate, got a taxi and left and never went back.

So that was a bit naughty! I should have told them I was leaving. But I didn't. I just scarpered.

When I worked at 'La Gavroche' for the Roux brothers, we used to have these beautiful chocolate truffles. The waiters were never allowed to eat these truffles under any circumstances. They were just for the customers.

But we noticed that some of the senior management, at the end of the night, if there were any left, they were eating them.

So, I was on a night shift one night. I came in about ten-thirty, just when they were usually putting out the left-over chocolate truffles. I got a syringe and filled it with blue food colouring. Then I injected these truffles with blue food colouring, because I knew that the managers would be eating them later on.

And there they were, walking back into the restaurant, looking after people, and they had bright blue mouths, and they didn't realise. I just went around with a smile on my face, knowing what I'd done.

Needless to say, the lowly waiters were allowed to eat the left-over chocolates too, after that. Nobody knew it was me.

I've never done anything really naughty at work. I've always tried to be very professional. I'll have a bit of a laugh and I say the wrong thing sometimes, without realising it.

I still do, to this day. What comes out of my mouth is what I'm thinking. Sometimes I think afterwards: "Have I just said that?" I know the staff here say sometimes: "Only you could get away with that."

Chapter 8

I used to get a lot of tips in London. Ex-Prime Ministers, for example.

I used to work at this restaurant that had a little booth that had a curtain round so they could sit having dinner with people that they shouldn't be having dinner with, which was always quite interesting.

I used to get a fifty-pound note pushed into my hand. That was for me to keep quiet about them being at the restaurant.

Talking of Prime Ministers reminds me of another job I did. One of my friends went to live with Carol Thatcher. Everybody in London rents out a room, to help pay the bills, and one of my friends was renting a room in her house. I went to help him get set up for a party that Carol was having.

Carol was walking around in this flamboyant dressing gown and there was a knock on the door so I answered it. I didn't think who was going to be the other side of that door, but it was her mother.

In walked Mrs Thatcher with Dennis behind her, carrying trays of food. They'd been to collect the food that Carol had ordered.

Mrs Thatcher just sat on this bar stool in the kitchen and she was talking. It was just after the time of the Brighton bombing. She had a very lucky escape, and she made a joke of it. Her words were: "If I hadn't been sat on the loo I'd be dead by now."

So being on the loo saved her from being blown up. She said; "I've dined out on that one for years." She was an interesting lady, very forceful – just like her daughter.

I got into trouble when I was working on another job at '47 Park Street' in London, when I waited on Antonio Banderas. There were serviced apartments within the hotel and he was staying there when he was working on 'Evita'.

I took up breakfast one morning. He was walking around in his underwear as I was setting the up table, putting on the cloth and all the china and a silver cloche over his breakfast.

He walked past me in his little pants and I just reached out and pinched his bottom as he went by. I couldn't resist the urge. He turned round and grinned but his manager, Deborah, told me off!

I did get a Christmas card from him after that and we still keep in touch.

One of the best tips I ever got in London was from his wife, Melanie Griffith. Their nanny let them down and Melanie gave me a thousand pounds to look after their two children for the day.

I took them to an art gallery because they were American and that's want they wanted to do in London. We had a spot of lunch and had ice cream. I'd only spent a hundred pounds because we'd been to places that didn't cost a lot of money but they'd had a wonderful time.

When we got back I gave Melanie the rest of the money but she said: "Oh, no. That's yours!" So that was quite a good tip.

I stood in a lift with Michael Jackson once. I was told by his minders I wasn't allowed to talk to him. I hadn't realised he was going to be in the lift. I just got in and saw him.

I said: "I admire you." And he looked back and smiled. I didn't really have a conversation with him, but it was nice.

As a waiter, you do come across a lot of celebrities. Everybody's got to eat, after all!

I met Elizabeth Taylor a few times, and Madonna, and Richard Gere, when I was in

America. He was lovely. And I met Patrick Swayze and John Travolta and Jon Bon Jovi.

I went to the opening of 'Planet Hollywood' in London and met Bruce Willis.

I had to look after Robin Williams at table one evening. Not the same voice came out of his mouth twice that night. Everything he said was in a different character. He was constantly someone else. Very strange . . .

I would have loved to meet some of the film stars from the era that I love but they've probably all died!

I'm sure I've met famous people without realising I've met them. They're just normal people when they're not in the limelight. A lot of the time, they don't like being in the limelight so you see a different side of them when you see them in private life.

When I worked at 'The Waltons', in Nottingham, we used to have the cast of 'Boon' in – Michael Elphic, Neil Morrissey. Shirley Bassey used to stay there and Honor Blackman. All the stars from Central TV, as it used to be, went there.

One-to-one they were all just normal, lovely, sometimes quite shy, ordinary people. As soon as an audience came in, they changed. It was very interesting to see.

And I can relate to that because I can be very insular and quite happy having an evening on my own. Then as soon as I'm in front of the public I start to put on an act.

Chapter 9

When I was in London I did a bit of acting – 'extra' work mainly. Twice I auditioned for 'East Enders', and 'The Bill', but I didn't get the parts. It would have been nice in a way, but I don't know if I would have been able to stand the life.

At the time, the actress whose house I lived in was always 'resting' and I thought: "I don't want this. I don't want a life of 'resting'." I wanted to earn my bread and butter and make sure I was earning all the time.

I did some modelling, too. That was entirely by accident.

Someone came into the place where I was working at the time and said: "Will you do a photo shoot for us?" I said: "Yes, I'll have a go."

So I went along and did this photo shoot and got paid five hundred pounds for doing it.

Then all of a sudden, two weeks later, I went to catch a bus and found my picture all over the bus stop. In fact, I was on the bus stops all the way down The King's Road.

Well, I did a lot of walking that week because I was too embarrassed to get in the bus queue!

And then I got a cheque for another five

hundred pounds because they'd made so much money out of it. So I thought to myself: "Okay. I quite like the idea of this."

I did a little bit of cat walk, too, but I don't think I'd be able to do it now – apart from hats and gloves!

I went to one catering job in London at a private house that needed a bit of acting skill. It was a huge place. It looked like a multi-storey hotel. We were doing a party for the daughter of the owner. When we got there we were told to go into this room and get changed.

I said: "I'm already wearing my black suit." But we were told no, we had a special outfit to wear. It turned out we had to change into leather G-strings and nothing else!

That's how we had to walk round all evening, serving trays of cocktails to all the guests. I could have won an Oscar that night.

I have to say, it was the old ladies who paid the most attention to the waiting staff!

When you need to earn a living to pay for your expensive life style, you do anything to get the money.

Some things are proper, some aren't!
I have to say, we got paid very well for that job.

Then one day I suddenly woke up and realised that I was going down the wrong path.
I decided to focus more seriously on my work.

When I went to London my ambition was to work in as many different styles of catering as possible. I started in the wine bars. I wanted to do the fast food, I wanted to do the fine dining.

I wanted to do everything. And by getting my

priorities sorted out, while I was in London,

I eventually managed to do that.

The boy at the bus stop on the King's Road

With Paul

Driving myself into the ground, attending events

The day I got the keys to Madhatters

Chapter 10

My other dream was to go to America and work on the cruise ships. So that's what I then did - I went out to America and worked on the ships cruising out of California.

When I first went to America we were flown over to California. The night before we embarked on the cruise ship we were put into a hotel in L.A.

They said we'd be picked up in the morning at 7.30am, so the night before, I went for a walk around outside.

Suddenly a police car came up beside me and the policeman said: "Get in."

I said, "No, I'm okay, I'm just having a walk." And he repeated: "Get in." I was about to say no again, and he said: "I'm not going to tell you a third time. Get in!"

So I got in the car and as we drove away someone got shot on the opposite corner. The policeman turned to me and said: "That's why I told you to get in."

I'd walked into the roughest, most dangerous part of L.A. which was quite scary, because it wasn't that far from where the cruise ships were going, and posh people were staying. I think that's when I decided I wasn't going to stay in the U.S. for long.

One group of people I met over in America, were called 'The BBW's' that stands for 'The Big Beautiful Women'.

These ladies were enormous – and I mean enormous. I was looking after them at a conference. There were a lot of different groups of women who had all come together for this annual conference or convention, all supporting each other.

I found it quite amazing that there was a group of people like this who were all so huge.

The lady who was in charge of them was so big she wasn't able to have her own room. She had to sleep in the conference room in a specially imported bed, she was that big. She ran the conference from her bed.

The Americans eat an awful lot. There was a buffet with food constantly available, and there was food coming to this woman 24/7. I very much doubt that lady is still with us now.

I remember taking one meal to her on a trolley. There were five beef burgers in this burger, garnished with salad, and a huge pile of chips. She said she had to eat her salad first because it was good for her. I just had to smile.

My job was to serve her meal and leave her to it. It wasn't for me to comment.

It's like that in night clubs as well, with excessive alcohol. You see people arrive looking glamourous and by the end of the night they have their shoes in their hand and they're falling down drunk. I've seen some very sorry sights but you can't say anything.

I left a really good job in London that paid really good money, to go to the States. I learned that when you go to America, no matter what level of management you were on before, when you get on the ships you begin at the bottom.

You start as a bus boy and work your way up. Your first job is clearing the dirty dishes.

And it's hard work. Nobody can tell me they've done a hard day's work if they haven't worked on the cruise ships. I worked from 5 in the morning until gone 2 in the morning, seven days a week with very few breaks. It's such hard work.

They were mainly Americans on the ships. But by an amazing co-incidence, on the other side of the word, on one of the ships I did meet a man who went to school with my father, which was quite incredible. He took a photo of me and when he got back to England he went round to see my parents.

He knocked on their door and said: "I've seen your lad and he's doing all right."

When I was working on one of the cruise ships Whoopi Goldberg was a passenger. She and I got into difficulties over a pot of jam.

Now, you have to understand the difference between the English language and the American language.

In English jelly is 'jelly', but in American it's called 'jello'. Americans call jam 'jelly'. I don't think they have anything called jam.

One day Whoopi Goldberg asked me for jelly, so I went and got her a little pot of jam.

"No, you stupid, English fool," she cried, "I wanted jello!"

She said it with a smile on her face, because knowing I was English, she had translated American 'jello' into English 'jelly' for my benefit.

I had then translated American 'jelly' into English 'jam' and brought her that, which was exactly what she didn't want!

But we got there in the end, and she got her jello.

Something I missed in California – it was always sunny! I missed the weather. I love the English weather. I love the seasons.

It was great fun to go, and something I had always wanted to do, but I didn't do it for long.

America is a long way away, especially the west coast.

I was too far from home. I missed being able to get on that train to go and see Mum and Dad.

Chapter 11

So, I came home. After I got back I decided to get somewhere on my own. I didn't want to go back and live with Mum and Dad.

So I found myself a new job and a new home and made a fresh start in Lincoln. And that was wonderful because that's where I met my partner, Paul.

I met him at Skegness – well, Chapel St. Leonard's actually – that sound's better than Skeg, doesn't it!

I was working at the Yew Lodge at Kegworth and one of the waitresses said to me: "You need to come away for the weekend with me."

So I went for an August Bank Holiday weekend to Chapel St. Leonard's.

I'd never been to that part of the world before. I couldn't believe the sea of mobile homes and caravans.

I walked into this little caravan that she had and met Paul and it was just amazing.

Paul was a singer. We went to see him singing on stage that night, and that was it.

Paul and I had a wonderful life together. We had a new home in Lincoln and I felt like I was putting my roots down again.

It wasn't flash. It was a proper bit of reality. It was an old airman's house just outside of Lincoln.

It was our little home in a lovely little village. Lincoln itself is beautiful. I absolutely loved it there.

That's when we got the dog, Sammy – that I've still got. He's old now, bless him. That represents a very happy part of my life.

It was a wonderful few years. I moved around between jobs, always looking for more, always looking for something else in the working environment. Nobody ever did it how I wanted it done.

I got a cracking job in the Vale of Belvoir and moved over there, to a flat above the hotel, still with Paul. From there I went for a very short stint in Loughborough and from there to Rutland, near Uppingham, which is a beautiful area.

All my jobs have a home included, so I just up sticks and move everything. That's got up sides and down sides. If everything works out, it's fine. But if it doesn't for some reason, then you've lost your home as well as your job.

I moved to Uppingham in the October. Paul had done a summer season and had gone to stay with his mum while I organised the new place.

The flat was full of boxes because I'd moved from a three-bedroom Victorian house into a one-bedroom flat.

It was in Uppingham, in an old thatched building. It was nice but very small.

And before we'd got properly settled in Paul was killed in a car accident in the December. And that was just the end of my life.

The owners of the place where I lived and worked were incredible. They took me under their wing and looked after me, all over the Christmas period.

At the beginning of February my sister gave birth to a little boy, which brought new life into the family and was lovely. But just at that time, the owners told me they were selling up.

So I'd lost my partner, my job and my home within a couple of months.

Then, I moved back to a place near to my mum and dad.

Chapter 12

I didn't want to actually move back in with my parents, but be close to them.

Thanks to the family that I have, they all rallied round and all clubbed together and sorted me out with somewhere to live. I got a little flat in Long Eaton.

I didn't know what to do, workwise, in the area. I was just stuck. Jobs, when I first started out, were so easy to come by but not now.

But I wasn't out of work for long.

I went from one, to another, to another as I had done before, always looking for something different, something interesting.

Then I got my dream job, at the time. I got to run a boutique hotel. That was the only box I hadn't ticked on my wish list.

I went to work at Woodborough Hall. I was still living in Long Eaton. I loved the job so much, but the commute was a bit far.

So I thought: "I'll get somewhere in the village." So I moved to Woodborough village.

By this time, it was a nearly three years since Paul had died.

I moved to Woodborough village in the October and the following February, Brian walked into my life.

I was sitting in the foyer at a cinema waiting for a friend, and Brian was sitting there waiting for his friend. We shared a table. We chatted.

Neither of our friends turned up . . . so that was that . . . We were just stuck with each other!

I carried on working at Woodborough Hall. Although it was three years since I'd lost my partner, I was still grieving. I'd tried to cope with the depression by working my way out of it, which was foolish.

I worked seven days a week, six in the morning until midnight. I had pressure on me from everywhere.

Finally, in October 2009, I had a heart attack, on the back seat of a bus.

It was brought on by stress. That was a wake-up call. That's what brought me to Kimberley.

I was told by Brian: "Leave the job. Come and live in Kimberley." And I did. And I've never looked back.

I'd never heard of Kimberley, never been there, and when I moved into the area I knew nobody, except Brian of course.

And this little town has given me so much. I've not just put down roots, they're growing rapidly. I'm not moving anywhere else now.

Inevitably, the illness struck again. I was suffering severe depression. I didn't go out of the house. The longest time I didn't leave the house was nearly three months. I would only accept phone calls from people I knew. That is not a good place to be. I don't ever want things to be like that again.

It was tough on my family. And on Brian, of course.

He was just incredible. He said: "Don't worry about working. Don't worry about anything. Just get better."

And with love, care and time, I did.

We know how to do celebrations! Christmas (left) and First Birthday events (right) at Madhatters. Believe it or not, that is a real cake (on the right!)

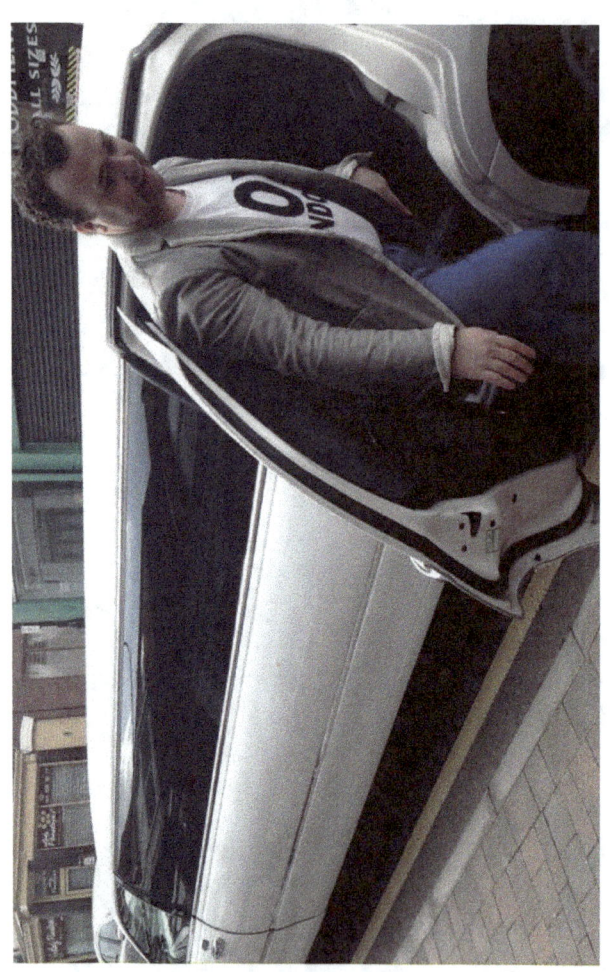

The Mad Hatter never draws attention to himself – as if I would!

Nice car. Not sure who that bloke is.

Chicken tonight, anyone?

Chapter 13

I could see, from 'Alice's Antiques, Crafts and Collectables', what a big appeal there was to the public from this kind of merchandise. I had the idea of running a 'Vintage and Craft Fair' on a Sunday in the Parish Hall.

Like most of my bright ideas, I wasn't sure whether it would take off or not so I mentioned it on social media. I got so many replies back, from potential stall holders and people who said they would come and buy, that it definitely seemed worth giving it a try.

That first one was so successful that I'm now doing three 'Vintage and Craft Fairs' a year. The first one is just before Mother's day, the second one is in the school holidays and the third one in the run up to Christmas.

I love them! They are like a travelling circus that just turns up and gives a wonderful day's entertainment, and then vanishes.

Kimberley Parish Hall is big and light and spacious. I get there about 7.30am when it's all swept clean and quiet and empty. I check that everything is laid out as I want it.

By arranging the tables so that people are guided round in a particular route, it's possible to get the maximum number of traders in the hall.

Then I go round and put the stall-holders'

names on their tables. In the summer we have outside pitches as well.

About an hour later the first vehicles start to turn up. Those coming the furthest usually arrive first. One is a vintage caravan. It stands on the car park with its awning out, reminding everyone of sea-side summer holidays when they were young!

Before long, everyone is piling in with boxes and trolleys, unpacking and setting out their wares. There is so much imagination in what people bring, and the way they display it. I'm fascinated to see the whole thing grow as the hall fills up.

All the craft items have to be made by the person selling them – I insist on that. I don't allow anything bought-in, ready made.

The variety always amazes me. We have beautiful sewn and knitted goods, beads and silver jewellery, jam and honey, dog treats, teddy bears, cup cakes, candles, books, wedding favours, ceramics and greetings cards.

Then there are the unexpected stalls, like the one selling exquisite miniature paper creations, or ornaments all made out of Lego, or ingredients in a jar to bake your own cookies.

And, of course, the 'Vintage' traders bring everything from hat pins to pith helmets. It's like Aladdin's cave.

We have an entertainer, too, a young lady who performs songs from all eras, with a touch of vintage in her choice of music.

We were lucky with the weather at our

last summer Fair. More than six hundred people came through the door. I don't think anyone passed the vintage ice cream van without getting a cornet!

At the pre-Christmas Fair we spread out on to the neighbouring streets. We had a hot roast chestnut stall and across the way from him, there was a hog roast. Somebody was wandering about handing out mince pies.

A lot of the small, local shops opened. There were more people about on the street that Sunday than there sometimes are on a regular shopping day.

It takes a lot of organising but it's brilliant when people come and enjoy it so much.

Chapter 14

Being 'The Mad Hatter' means to me being part of the community. I may be totally eccentric – in a way that not everybody likes – but I aim to attract as much fun as possible. If I can make one person happy every day by being this eccentric, mad character in my tea shop, then I've achieved my goal.

Money has never driven me. I was earning mega money in London, but I was spending mega money, like it was going out of fashion. But it's never been the be all and end all to me. As long as I can pay my way, pay my bills, and something for me, then I'm happy.

I think sitting round a table having tea is very civilised and far more sociable and far more pleasurable than drinking alcohol. Plus, you can get in the car afterwards and you don't have to worry about drink-driving. I don't think they're going to invent a breathalyser for tea.

In the last three years, since I opened Madhatters, it's made me feel part of the community and I like to participate in every way I can.

In May 2014 we had a big event in Kimberley when the Royal Engineers marched through the town in a 'Freedom of Entry' parade. It was very spectacular, with 150 soldiers and veterans involved, plus a military band.

Our local M.P., Anna Soubry, was Parliamentary Under-Secretary of State for Defence at the time, with special responsibility for Personnel, Welfare and Veterans, so she took a great interest in the 'Freedom of Entry' parade.

The whole town was out on the street to see them march from our war memorial – which is a unique structure and very unusual – to a big, open-air church parade in Hall Om Wong open space.

The top brass took the salute at the crossroads just by my old tea shop, so we went to town and decorated the outside of the premises with sandbags and camouflage, to make it look like a dug-out. I dressed up in military fatigues and tried to look like a lean, mean, fighting machine.

There were real soldiers stewarding the parade who looked as if they pumped iron five hours a day. And you could have cut yourself on their creases!

Again, it was a beautiful day weather-wise so the whole event went off very well.

Our M.P. is very supportive of small businesses and she has been kind enough to take some notice of Madhatters. She chose the old tea shop to hold a Saturday morning surgery for constituents on one occasion.

Twice, she has included my staff on visits to the Houses of Parliament in London, which has been a very nice reward for them for all the work they put in. We were given a conducted tour of the Palace of Westminster, which was very interesting and memorable.

The local reporter from 'The Nottingham Post' regularly sits in the tea shop to meet people who wanted to come and tell him a story or ask him to research something for them.

The 'Post' and our weekly newspaper 'The Eastwood and Kimberley Advertiser' have been very supportive. We get a lot of mentions, and Nygel in a funny hat is always good for a photo!

I've been invited to take part in a number of live discussions on 'BBC Radio Nottingham'. That's always good fun. I just have to be careful my mouth doesn't run away with me and I blurt out something I wish I hadn't said!

'Notts TV' came in to film in the tea shop and got some priceless footage of the tiny tots having tea. It's all about the customers, not about me.

I was very pleased to be asked to organise a 'black tie' charity event on behalf of The Mayor of Broxtowe's chosen charities in 2013.

One was The Royal British Legion. The other was The Ryan Lee Trust.

This local charity is named for a young school boy who very sadly passed away as a result of a number of brain tumours. His parents now fundraise to provide essential aids for other young sufferers that they were not aware of when Ryan was being treated, but which would have helped him.

We had a spectacular evening at The Kimberley Institute Cricket Club and raised an amazing amount.

I've done other things for charity over the years. This year I've shaved my head and before that I've shaved my legs. I've never been one to be able to say no to a charity do.

When, quite a long while ago, I was asked to wear a dress on a charitable night to raise funds for the Terrence Higgins Trust, I said yes.

So I worked one night with Lily Savage, who was Paul O'Grady's 'alter ego'.

Interestingly, as a person Paul was very quiet, even quite shy, but as soon as the costume went on, he changed. And I could relate to that. When you're dressed up like that, you become somebody else.

In this double-act with Lily Savage, I was called 'Letta Av-it' and I wore a black dress with a white wig.

There was a coach full of children all

dressed as page boys and fairies that went round the auditoriums of the West End theatres with collecting buckets.

We did this act, with one of us on the stage and the other one in the audience. It was after the interval but before the second half of the show. We managed to do about three in the one night. We had a ball and we raised thousands.

I'd never done anything like that before. I'd got a bra to wear under my dress and I'd been told to get chicken fillets to put down my bra to fill it out. So I went and got these chicken fillets.

My actress friend, whose house I lived in, told me where to get them. She said: "You'll get them in Marks."

At the end of the night we went out for a few drinks, as you do.

I thought: "Well, I'm in a frock, I might as well make a night of it."

So we went round the West End. I got home, and my actress friend was still up, with one of her friends. She said: "How have you done, then?"

I said: "I've got to take these chicken fillets out. They're really slimy." She said: "Where did you go to get them?" I said: "Where you told me – Marks & Spencers on Baker Street."

I'd been to the food hall and bought fresh chicken breast fillets. What I should have done was go to the underwear department and buy silicone bra boosters, that they call 'chicken fillets' because that's what they look like. They're proper hygienic bust enhancers.

But I didn't know that. I bought the real thing. At least I didn't buy frozen ones!

Anyway, these fresh chicken fillets I'd got down my bra were about cooked by this time — I'd been wearing them all night and I was that hot. But they'd done the job. They looked okay.

We fed them to the cat next day.

Chapter 15

Since I've become 'The Mad Hatter' and been running the tea shop business, I've met a lot of people who have become friends, which is lovely.

I feel as if I've put my roots down in a place where I feel loved and cared for. And I feel I can return that, as well. I'm enjoying the friendship, the fun, the community that I've got within this environment that I've created.

In Kimberley and this area I fit like a little piece of a jigsaw puzzle.

I'm self-motivated. I've always been up at the crack of dawn and doing. As a child, I was playing with toys or cars, or making my farm. If the sun was shining: "Can I go out?" I was always wanting to do something. It's natural for me to motivate myself – nobody else is going to do it.

There are potential projects on the horizon. I feel as though I laid the foundations when I started this business three years ago. I've now put a good few courses of bricks around.

Now, I just need to gradually build slowly until I move on to the next project. So far as location is concerned, living, being and doing in this area, I'm very settled. What comes next, well, I don't know.

I never stand still. I've always got ideas for new things.

My core, personal priority is that life stays as it is, blossoms and continues blossoming.

The business life could either stay at the same sort of level, just going along nicely, or it could go 'boom!' and explode. At the moment, I think what I have works very nicely alongside my private life and it's getting that work-life balance right that is important.

Getting it right for me and for the others around me. I need to make sure everybody else is all right. In my world, I'm responsible for everybody around me being happy – my staff, my customers, my family. If everyone has got a smile on their face, 'The Mad Hatter' is happy.

www.ingramcontent.com/pod-product-compliance
Lightning Source LLC
Chambersburg PA
CBHW071007080526
44587CB00015B/2381